But It Only Happened Once

Valuable, Priceless, Real Life Experiences for Everyday Teen Choices!

Joy Henley

PublishAmerica
Baltimore

First printing

ISBN: 1-59129-762-1
PUBLISHED BY PUBLISHAMERICA BOOK PUBLISHERS
www.publishamerica.com
Baltimore

Printed in the United States of America

Dedication

Sometimes when we go through an ordeal, we do not realize we have been given a gift. The Lord chose me to be the recipient of a gift. The life experiences I have endured had a purpose. With His divine wisdom and grace, I humbly try to make a difference. I know I am supposed to share what I have learned—no matter how humiliating. It would be selfish to keep all I have learned to myself. I have had many life experiences for a reason. It took me awhile to realize that God must focus on me often. He has given me tremendous life experiences, no doubt believing that I can not only handle them, but also grow to help others. This book is dedicated to The Lord Above.

A Special Thank You

I would like to thank PublishAmerica for believing in, and publishing *But It Only Happened Once*. It took a special publisher to not only see the need for this book, but to print it. Their belief and interest in young people, and myself as an author, is much appreciated.

Special Acknowledgment

To Justin—for such incredible computer assistance! The magnet on my refrigerator says, "Everything I learned about computers, I learned from my kid," and it certainly is the truth!

My mother and brother for always being there!

To the many teens who helped to provide the inspiration for this book!

I would also like to give tribute to someone who is very wise, and through our conversations, has helped me to grow spiritually. Every church should have a pastor like Gary R. Jepsen.

Introduction

Thinking of having sex? How will you pay for it? There is a price, in case you didn't know! Oh…you thought you were just going to use her, have some fun and then dump her? Well, it doesn't quite work like *that*! Maybe she is going to use you to conceive a child. She wants a baby and she has decided she will just have you support the baby! You don't think you are going to run, do you? You will just say the baby is not yours? You aren't going to pay child support because you don't have it? This is the adult world now and you are going to be treated as a parent. Don't worry if you have not been very responsible up to this point…the law will help you now.

There are some things you just cannot learn in class. Textbooks do not contain all of the answers. There are some results and outcomes in life that even Mom and Dad cannot predict. Some of us learn the hard way. We walk the really tough road, and although the lessons are painful, the growth is tremendous. When I told people I was going to write about *this*, well…let's just say they thought I had lost my mind!

There will be no boring statistics or endless preaching here. I am not going to talk "at" you. I am going to shock you though! Really shock you. Believe me, even the most talented writer could not create the happenings you are about to read within these pages. Will you read this and soon forget? Not on your life! This is a powerful non-fiction book, filled with consequences, outcomes and end results.

You are probably wondering what qualifies me to write about such a horrendous subject. I am not a famous celebrity and I am not wealthy. I have not spent years studying this topic nor have I taken tests. No, my education far exceeds this. I am an expert. In many ways, I am more educated regarding life experiences than a worldly scholar or someone on an honor roll. The difference between them and me is that I have *lived* this. I promise you that no rehearsal, no exam, or instructor could prepare me for such education.

In high school, my friends and I were invincible and we lived by the popular motto: *It will never happen to ME*. Tragedy happens to others. My high school boyfriend's partying seemed cool. He was so popular and so handsome, with the world before him! I never planned to see him lying in a coffin a few months after graduation. Suddenly, partying was no longer the "in" thing, and we grew up fast! Partying—mixing alcohol with sleeping pills can cause a heart attack. It wasn't supposed to happen to him.

No one could prepare me to have five pregnancies, yet only raise one child to happy, healthy adulthood. I never dreamed a court could strip a loving, kind, caring mother of her dignity…and her child. I never dreamed one false allegation—just one lie by a vindictive ex-partner can cause a child to live in abuse for years to come. I just never knew. I never imagined that I would pay thousands of dollars to a child abuser—the man who beat my child. I never could fathom living 14 years without my child. I could never dream that my own child could be set up or orchestrated to tell lies about me—his mother—to a court. I certainly never dreamed that his stories would be believed. Life is supposed to be fair! What happened?

These are examples of life experiences. They are painful, but they are our best teachers. It is through these life experiences that we achieve our greatest growth.

It was just one wrong choice in a partner, but it cost me. It would haunt me, provoke me, humble me, strip me of my self-esteem, challenge my faith and my sanity. It would touch and assault innocent people. It would be my teacher. One day I would learn from it and be able to help others.

"One day" is now. It is time. Whether I humor, anger, or startle you, you are going to feel *something*. Long after you turn the final page, you will be thinking of this book as a tool for life.

Get ready because you have never read anything like *this*!

Let's talk *Life Experiences*!

Chapter 1

Tonight is the night! You have planned it for weeks, you have prepared to make it perfect, it is finally going to happen! The two of you are going to be together…not "together" for a class, not "together" for dinner, or for a movie. You are going to be together in the way that counts. Tonight…you come together, in your dreams, your passion, your ecstasy…as one. The scenario is perfect. His parents are out of town. You can't miss this time, and how could anything go wrong? With his parents 800 miles away, he has the house to himself. It is a big secret—not even your friends know about tonight. (Well, you did tell your best friend, but she will keep the secret until the day she dies!) You have remembered the music, the breath mints, the exquisite perfume, and the sexy lingerie. You don't need a checklist for this one! You know exactly what will turn him on! After tonight, he will love you forever. Once you give yourself to him in all of your passion, he will never forget you. The act of lovemaking will bond you forever. Take one more look around…have you forgotten something? There is one thing. Look at his picture. Look close. Stare into his eyes. **WOULD YOU BE WILLING TO DIE FOR HIM?** Oh, and there is one other question…do you have **$180,000**? This is how much money it will require in basic costs, for you to raise your child, should you become pregnant on this magical night. You better have money—or the means to come up with it. You better be willing to give up your professional or career dreams. Your job at Taco Time will not cover it! Actually now that I think about it, basic costs are just that…“basic.” So, just plan on having a quarter of a million dollars when you conceive a child!

Do you love him or her enough to die?

Are you willing to risk a lifetime of “breakouts,” inflammation, or disease for this *one* sex act?

Are you ready to sleep with every person your partner has slept with?

Are you willing to give up your dreams for this person? Do you honestly believe it won’t happen to you?

What is it about your partner that makes you feel safe? Perhaps your partner is handsome, beautiful, clean, and claims to use birth control. Maybe your partner is using protection and maybe not. There could be an attack! They have no voice and they strike with no warning. They lurk, they wait, and they can attack you!

Tonight…the mood may be passion. On another day, mysterious symptoms appear. Yes, it could be the “flu”…or it could be the beginning of a battle to save your life.

Some STDs are curable, some are treatable, and some are fatal. Should you be infected with HIV tonight, this can evolve into full-blown AIDS. Don’t even think…*IT WON’T HAPPEN TO ME!*

Birth control is supposedly simple! It is everywhere!

It's quick, disposable, it's cool! Pop a pill! Insert a vaginal suppository! Use contraceptive film! Just grab one of the pills that have set in the bottom of your purse for days. (I am being sarcastic—you can't just suddenly take a birth control pill as needed.) He promises he will hopefully apply the condom at the right moment! You will just leave the birth control stuff to your partner. Big mistake! Take responsibility for your choices and body. The only way you can be sure birth control is not only used—but used appropriately—is to do it yourself. No one would ever say birth control is useless! Well, let me be the first! YOUR BIRTH CONTROL IS USELESS...*unless you use it correctly, per instruction.*

First, no birth control (even "the pill") is 100% effective. You must be committed to taking birth control pills every day—without fail. It must be part of your daily routine—hopefully the pill will be taken at approximately the same time each day. This is a good habit! Condoms must be applied correctly—it is easy for some semen to overflow. Condoms fall off, and sometimes end up inside the woman. Perhaps he is one of those guys who just does not like to wear condoms. Guys say it hampers the sexual performance and besides, like one guy says, "I just don't like the feel of it." He doesn't like "the feel of it"? Well, we can see how he will like the "feel" of paying child support for the next 18 years, of having his income garnished, and providing for his child. There are guys who will tell you to take a hike if you insist they must wear a condom. They insist it is the only way they will have sex. He is not worth playing Russian Roulette with your life!

Let him have sex with someone else who is willing to gamble with their life! Say good-bye! You deserve better!

Do not jeopardize your health for anyone! I guarantee you, you will probably have HIV or Herpes long after he is gone.

You will lose him? What have you lost? A person who does not give a darn about your feelings or health? A person who is going to be in control of the relationship? A person who only is concerned with *his* pleasure? Wake up…this is not love! This is selfish and uncompromising, not to mention irresponsible and immature. If you have to sleep with him to "keep him," you did not have him in the first place! Sex should be a mutual decision—something that makes both of you feel comfortable. It cannot be that satisfying if you are worried because he will not use protection. Well…at least he is not as weird as some of those guys on the TV talk programs. It's not like he is one of those guys who pokes holes in the condom and laughs!

Believe it or not, there are men who love to keep a woman pregnant. There is an old saying called "barefoot and pregnant," and there are chauvinistic men who like to "spread their seeds around" as one young lady told me. If he can keep you "barefoot and pregnant" or being a "baby machine," you will not venture out into the career world—or at least not initially. You will be too busy to plan a career—you will be changing diapers, cleaning spit up and vomit and being up all night with a howling baby. You will not have many friends and barely have enough time to see your family. Without a job, you will have no money to call your own. You will be dependent on him for every cent. You will ask for money, justify the need for it, and explain your purchases. He may go out and party, meet other women, or abuse you. He can laugh and ponder *what are you going to do about it*? Sadly, you are going to tolerate it, and do absolutely nothing. What would you do? Leave him? How would you feed the baby, and provide for every need? Do you honestly believe your partner would have respect for you? When a woman is dependent on the baby's father—to an extreme—I call this a "set-up." In other words, it is designed so one of you has the power in the relationship. It is not an equal relationship, by any means.

Abusers are big at impregnating their women—the more children she has—the more dependent she is. He then has more control, and it is nearly impossible for her to leave. The chances of you departing such a set-up diminish with each birth, and each act of abuse—whether it be emotional, physical or sexual. The thing that will really take a beating is your self-esteem. Your world will become small—taking care of the baby. He will also expect you to keep him happy because, after all, he works. Your 24-hour a day childcare is not seen as "work" by him. He brings home the money, he is tired when he gets home, and he feels you owe him. He sees himself as working a "real job." It is like he does you a favor when he works and provides for you and the baby. You are stuck—you are in a rut. How are you going to get out of it? You will have to pay an attorney legal fees. Where will you come up with *that* money?

There are men who are on the hunt for a woman with no goals, no ambition and who is ready to produce an heir or offspring for him. They will target a woman like this, and have a sort of built-in "radar" when it comes to finding her! If a woman is educated, goal-oriented, selective due to her high self-respect, values her health, and pays attention to the subtle cues that this man is a "macho and control" type person, this scenario probably would not happen in the first place. A creep like this would not ever even stand a chance of attracting her attention!

Chapter 2

Those sperm are plentiful, sneaky and they travel fast! We want to believe our partner is honest and trustworthy but unfortunately, people lie. Yes...even your sweetie is capable of telling a lie! Believing your partner is taking care of the birth control is not being responsible. Taking care of *you* is responsible. Do not leave this responsibility to someone else. He can use his condoms, while you use your preferred method of birth control. You can be tested for STDs. You can insist *he* be tested for STDs. What? He is insulted because you want him to take the test? You are afraid he will think you are weird and break up with you? If the other person objects to this, perhaps *that person* has a problem. To insist someone take an HIV or AIDS test prior to intercourse is taking care of both of you. It shows your partner that you have self-esteem and respect. Taking responsibility is cool! A couple was featured on television who wrapped their negative STD test results in colorful, curly ribbons. They had a cozy, fun celebration of their disease-free health and efforts to accept responsibility. It is cute...it's not dumb! This couple has class and they will live to see their dreams fulfilled. They are overflowing with respect for each other and proud of themselves.

While having sex with someone, how do you really know your partner is of legal age? There are many young men currently spending years in prison because the pretty, flirty, young lady told them she was 18 or 19. Hey guy…when the parents find out you had sex with their 16-year-old daughter, they can bring legal criminal charges against you. You *are* screwed! But…what happened? She looked older, she wore all of that make-up, and you believed she was 18. Well now, as you look back—and we all know "hindsight is 20/20," maybe she did look a bit younger. You are so confused. She just came onto you so strong…didn't you do what most guys would do? She was *asking* to go to bed with you—pleading, begging you with her hot body! Was the thrill of sex with her worth it? While in your jail/prison cell, you will repeatedly ask yourself this question. You could have years to contemplate it.

Many teenagers have become parents, all the while insisting, "but I didn't think it would happen to me." Why do each of us have this inner feeling that things will not happen to us exclusively? How is it that we are so above the consequences or so above the law? Wouldn't it be grand if each of us adopted the attitude that it *will* happen to us! Imagine how this would sway our decisions and change the course of our life. It's the *attitude*…and if you think you can have casual, frequent, unprotected sex and nothing is going to happen…you are dead wrong! It is time to grow up and get real!

I especially want to commend teens and those who believe in the sanctity of marriage. There are really couples out there who want to wait until their wedding night. This is old fashioned, romantic and priceless. As these teens will attest, abstinence works! There are once sexually active teens that are now taking "vows of celibacy." These teens do not care what their friends think, they do not need their friends' approval, and they do not need to sleep around to be cool. They are obviously strong in their own convictions and capable of standing up for their beliefs. In a time of raging hormones and sexual promiscuity, they are attempting to not act on their emotions. I do not have to tell you that this is not an easy thing to do. Yeah, it's not the "in" thing to do. Practically everyone has had sex...you almost feel like a freak, if you have not done it! 17 years old and a virgin? Unbelievable? I say...awesome! If both partners cannot responsibly use birth control, keep their legs together and private parts zipped up, guess what! Think about HIV turning into full-blown AIDS.

Remember...a quarter of a million dollars! Do you have the money, honey? Let's talk about having a baby. A precious, adorable baby to cuddle, to love. A baby to call your own...

Chapter 3

When I worked as a Para-Educator at the local high school, I overheard a student one morning. She was giggly and excited as she whispered to her classmates. The teacher finally stopped the classroom discussion and suggested that she share her good news with the class! She blurted, "I am going to have a baby…I am so excited! I am going to have a Gap Baby!" As she enthusiastically talked and beamed, she rubbed her tummy. She scribbled girl baby names on the outside of her theme book. "Marissa," "Courtney," "Amber." She promised the class that *nothing* would be too good for her baby. As she became enveloped in a whirlwind of discussion, another teacher muttered under her breath, "how is she going to have a Gap Baby? With her boyfriend's income at Taco Time"? This 15-year-old is about to enter the "School of Hard Knocks." Tuition is free. The "curriculum" is the toughest you will ever experience. When you are ready to "graduate," you will know it. If you graduate "with honors" you will feel like you have been to hell and back.

You are having a baby! Guess what! The world is no longer about you—your desires, your wants, your needs. Don't worry…you don't need a social life anyway! You will be too sleep-deprived to care! You will not be spending weekends at the mall, because you will not have the money, energy or time. You are going to be financially struggling, exhausted from being up with your baby at all hours, and you are now going to be on a strict feeding schedule. You will not determine your own breaks when you get tired or stressed out. You are now going to react to the sound of a "different drummer." It is a baby. This is a 24 hour a day commitment. While your friends are talking on the phone or going to the concert, you are going to make sure the bottles are sterilized and that there is a sufficient supply of diapers. Babies need clean clothes and you will get used to doing the continuous laundry.

Begin now by checking into medical and life insurance. Having a baby will cost thousands of dollars and you will need to pay the hospital. Without insurance, you will be required to pay cash for the mother and baby labor/delivery care (or set up a payment plan) before you leave the hospital. Budgeting and numbers may have been difficult for you in math class, but you will learn now. You have no choice because your child will fail to thrive if you do not carefully plan. You must now plan to purchase nutritious foods for you and your child. Now, the lingering, distant thought that the welfare office is only a few blocks away, plays in your mind. Go there…see how much welfare pays for one parent and one child. How will you even find a home with this meager amount of money? Enter and sign up so you and your baby can become a case number! Eventually, welfare will terminate you as this is not a forever thing. With a 5-year maximum life payment in some states, you will eventually work. You will then pay for childcare. Full-time infant childcare currently costs approximately $800.00 a month in Seattle. With paying rent, food, childcare, clothing, diapers, formula, etc. you are going to have to have a pretty high paying job. Where will you acquire the skills? School requires tuition, costs, books, etc. Now you move on to the next idea.

The father of the baby. He is out there, he cares, he promised to love you forever (especially when he was making love to you). You can always rely on him, right? Of course he told you he "loves" you…talk is cheap! When he must choose between his sports car and the baby, of course he is going to choose the baby, right? He will gladly fork over a percentage of his income for his child, right? You will hang onto him with all of your might because you have to depend on him. What if he walks? What if he finds someone else? We better have a talk with the dads.

What? The dad-to-be does not know if he wants this? He lied? He doesn't love you? He plans to go to school. He is not going to spend the rest of his life with you. You are not ready for this? You plan to dump her or run away? You can try it but you won't get far. You can dump her but you are not going to dump your responsibility which is now your child. Medical bills, child support, etc. now will come out of your paycheck. You don't make much? They will just take what you have. Who are "they?" Well, I am referring to the State Division of Child Support. If you do not want to fulfill your child support obligation, they will make you do so. You don't have a choice. It's the law that you will provide for your child. Did I mention that you will pay for the next 18 years? It does not seem fair when you consider that you were actually in bed for about an hour!

What are your options? You can marry the mother of your child. Do you love her? Are you in love with her? Maybe just in love with her body? Do you want to see her face for the next 18 years? Can you be true to only her? Are you willing to stop partying or hanging out on the weekends, and pour your heart and soul into making a home for your baby? You will work—college is now on hold because you have medical bills to pay and arrangements to make. You have a baby coming within months. If marriage is not something you care to do, then you may as well just walk into the State Division of Child Support. They want you…or let's say they want your money and they want it bad! They will find you. They are very good at what they do.

The Division of Child Support collects child support for the children in our state. When you father a child, your name will be placed into their computer system and they will come knocking. Your parents are not going to get you out of this one! Now stop laughing and making those ridiculous remarks like, "it's not *my* baby. She screwed around with at least 6 of my friends. Yeah…well, she can prove it!" If the mother does not prove it, the state will. Today's paternity tests are highly accurate. *You* are now the "parent" and you and DCS are now going to be chummy. What can DCS (Division of Child Support) do?

They will contact your employer to notify them you have a child support obligation. They can take a huge chunk of your income every month. They will keep track of your assets and income.

They will place a "lien" on any home you purchase—should you owe back child support. They will require you to pay for your child's health care, and daycare in addition to the monthly child support amount. If your child is receiving Public Assistance, they can order you to re-pay the State.

You just want to spend quality time with your child! You will have a visitation or Parenting Plan agreement, which outlines your schedule. To create this agreement with an attorney will cost you in attorney's fees. This can range from $150.00 to $500.00 an hour! There is just one realistic thought you need to keep in mind. This is a *piece of paper*. The other parent must comply to make it work. Should he or she refuse, this is called "Custodial Interference" in legal terms, and you will need to go back to court. Having plans outlined on paper is one thing…but having plans enforced is another!

I know a man who spent 10 years trying to see his child. He spent literally thousands of dollars on contempt motions, paying not only a several thousand dollar retainer fee but legal bill. He never did manage to see his child. You can ask why he did not call the police. He did—many times. They would look at the court order and say, "this is a matter for Family Court. You need to take her back to court." He did—for 10 years. For a custody matter, most legal professionals require a "retainer"—an upfront cost to begin working on your case, which usually requires $3500.00 (at least). A few years ago, a custody "battle"—

one with numerous allegations, many affidavits/ depositions, and attorney's fees—averaged $30,000.00. Add *this* to that $180,000.00 basic cost of raising your child to the age of 18! You will be lucky if you can afford to buy gas for your car! Actually, you might have to sell that car to pay your child support!

I am well acquainted with a gentleman—well okay, most females would call him a "hunk," or "drop dead gorgeous." He made love on the beach one night, one hot, steamy night, under the twinkling stars, a full moon, and amidst the passion in the air. Although he was drunk and does not precisely recall many of the details, he and the woman wanted it. They wanted it bad…so they wandered off from the party, away from the roaring fire, and got lost in the trees. They came to a small patch of beach sand and lay down. The man estimates he was with the woman "probably 20 minutes or so." When they were finished, they both kind of went their separate ways. She had been hanging around the party group by the fire, but was not actually known by anyone. She was just kind of there…lurking…waiting…wanting…what? What did she want? The man soon learned that she was on welfare, wanted to get pregnant and as he put it, "looking for a meal ticket."

For that "probably 20 minutes or so" on the beach, he paid for the next 18 years—actually beyond 20 years. When they parted on that heat ridden, summer night, he did not even know her name. He would soon know it well, because they were going to be connected. They conceived a human life that night. The woman somehow managed to locate this man, and he soon learned she was aggressive, demanding, possessive and desperate.

She told him she and the baby were now a "package deal" and that she was planning a life for them. She told him he did not have any choice—that they were going to be a family. She learned where the man worked. He would open his lunch box to find a baby picture she had somehow planted in it. Reminders were everyplace. She called at all hours, knocked on his door and threatened, "I am not going anywhere…I am the mother of your child."

She contacted his relatives, boasting to every family member how she was the mother of his child. Although he never married the woman, he watched his income be sliced in huge proportion, and be given to the mother of the child for child support. There is no doubt he upgraded the woman's lifestyle. She moved out of that welfare housing and into a luxurious condo. She squeezed him for every cent. When he got a raise at work, so did she. She was right there waiting in the wings…waiting to petition the court for more child support. Even when the child support was paid, she still needed more. He was responsible for the next 18 years.

After the 18 years when his mother and father died, she was lurking…waiting…again. (She seemed to have a knack for doing this!) She demanded money from the wills for their son. It turned into a major court battle. 20 minutes of lust…18 years of pay for the act. He is such a nice guy. Why him? He has asked himself this a zillion times!

Another young man I know fathered three children and his wife was tragically killed in a car accident. He did not want the responsibility of these children when he was married. He chose to go out with friends, party, have girlfriends, and place his fun as a priority. She took care of the children and was always there. If he did not want the responsibility of these children when he had a partner, he certainly would not want it now. Now, he would be both mom and dad. It was not supposed to be like this. He had it made—always doing "his" thing…the party is now over! Situations like his just go to show that even though you have a partner to "fall back on" or to accept a portion or most of your responsibility, it is not permanent. You will ultimately be responsible. It also shows that we never, really appreciate what or who we have in our lives until it is gone. Then, it is just too late. Too many people have learned this the hard way.

Life does not always go according to plan. I never meant to miscarry my twins. That certainly was not part of my plan. People who bring children into this world who are disabled did not plan it. I know of frustrated, exhausted parents who have children with behavior problems. Their lives are spent arguing, compromising, in counseling sessions and in tears. It was not supposed to be this way. Depending upon your circumstances, sometimes caring for one child can seem as hectic as caring for three! I know of parents who have spent years caring for children who required medical attention. Their 5-year-old does not act like other 5-year-olds—their 5-year-old is like a 1 1/2-year-old…diapers and all. Mothers and fathers change these diapers, spoon feed these children, bathe and nurture them.

A parent who has a child with such needs has a much

longer day than the rest of us. God bless every one of them too. Sometimes parenthood just is not what we anticipate. We ask…why me? Why my child? How will I do this? Dig deep into your heart and ask yourself how you would feel if you had a child with special needs. Would you, as that child's father, be equipped financially and emotionally to meet your child's needs? Be honest with yourself.

I have learned that as parents we do what we have to do. When I had to work two jobs to support my child, I did it. When I had to work three jobs, I did it. People criticized me for working. Suddenly, I was this neglectful mother because I worked and left my child. I was accused of choosing my job over my child. True, I did not get to spend much time with him, while working various jobs. I received very few pats on the back for providing a roof over his head, feeding and clothing him, and not running to the nearest welfare office. When an acquaintance heard I had just got off work from one job, and was headed for the second one he snarled, "in my country…we put family first." I looked at him and mumbled, "funny, that's what I thought I was doing." As parents, we have a built-in mechanism and energy reserve that assures us we can do anything we have to for our child. I quickly learned after giving birth, that I could stay up for two nights with a screaming, clinging baby, and go to work on the third morning. I learned to make it on 3 hours of sleep…and this was a good restful night, at times.

Whatever differences you and your partner have about child rearing, you better hope and pray that the two of you can work this out. The smart parents put their children first and foremost. I know…I know…you did not want all of this. You just wanted to have a few drinks, sex, and just "party." Your parents are worried sick. They did not plan on becoming grandparents this way and you love them so much. They look at you and your mother cries, "what about college?" The only way you can imagine coming up with the money you need, will be to use that college fund your parents saved and scrimped to give you. You have a responsibility now—at least for the next 18 years. Wasn't life easy when you only had to worry about who your date will be this Friday night, shopping at the mall, or attending a Cross Country meet?

Chapter 4

Fathers do not always pay support. As the mother, it may be up to you to pay child support to the father. Go ahead and think it could not happen to you. Just because you gave birth does not guarantee you will raise the baby to happy, healthy adulthood. Just because you are a kind, caring, wonderful mother does not guarantee you will have your child with you for years to come. The number of non-custodial mothers has risen significantly since the early 1980s. Many people have a stereotypical idea of what a non-custodial mother looks like. In your vision, she may be a drug addict or prostitute. She may be poor, living in her car, and have no one in the world. Are you wrong! Non-custodial mothers today are wise, educated, and career women. There are many reasons why a mother could be separated from her child. Some mothers choose to give up their children for adoption, other mothers lose their children when the father kidnaps the child, and some lose custody through unjust court rulings. Should the father decide he is the better parent, or re-marry, he could seek custody.

Alcoholics, drug dealers, prostitutes and child abusers are granted custody of children. Our legal system is not perfect and judges do make wrong decisions. Your friends can insist, "he's a drug dealer…no court in this land would give him custody," but justice does not always prevail.

The father is at a real advantage if he has a strong family unit supporting him. It will cost much money when the father petitions for custody. Should he bring allegations against you as a mother, you will have to defend yourself. Child abuse is a felony. Neglecting your child will surely result in the child being taken from you.

Spanking your child? Let's just say I have been personally acquainted with people who rarely spanked their children, but the few times they did, they were told they broke the law. Spanking or hitting your child can be viewed as an "assault" as a friend of mine discovered when she was charged with child abuse. She was handcuffed and taken out of her home to jail. It did not matter that her daughter had shoved her and called her a "fu--ing bit--." It did not matter that every time her brat daughter did not get her way, she would just go to the telephone and call Children's Protective Service with a false complaint of abuse.

The other parent of your baby, and grandparents can bring allegations, and the State can intervene with one anonymous call. His friends may be drunks or drug dealers but they can still make you look like a bad mother.

Anyone can phone C.P.S. and say you were yelling at your child (emotional abuse), spanking him or her (physical abuse), or touching your child's genitals (sexual abuse). True, you were giving the baby a bath and had to wash his scrotum and penis, but you can explain that later, in your lengthy, expensive court hearing. Personally speaking, when I put my 3-year-old's head under the bathroom faucet to wash his hair, his dad accused me of "trying to drown him." Yes, it's absurd, but judges, social workers and court officials listen to this stuff.

Should you be court-ordered to pay child support, it won't be easy. First—as a woman, you may find you earn less than a man. You will most likely be granted visitation with your child. Hope the father complies with the court order. Hope the father does not make false allegations against you. Hope the father does not re-marry and you have to watch another woman play mommy to your child.

I know of a woman who went to a Lactation Specialist so she could produce breast milk. What is so spectacular about this? She went through a series of breast exercises so she could breastfeed another woman's child! (The biological mother was a friend of mine.) This woman and the baby's biological father wanted custody of the baby. She would go to any lengths—even producing breast milk, to assume her "mommy" role. I know of mothers who have endured their children being kidnapped by the father, mothers who had custody here in my state—while the father went to another state and obtained custody, and mothers who have not seen their children in many years. Those custody disputes are downright nasty! If you are a non-custodial parent or have Family Law issues with the child's father, reach a compromise. Put your personal feelings of negativity and hostility aside and place your child's interests first.

In my personal situation, when I was a non-custodial parent, it quickly became a joke that "it will take a tow truck to move that file to another legal firm." A wise judge once made the comment, "you can judge how many emotional problems a child will have by looking at the thickness of the parent's Family Court file." Allegations and the consequent hearings can be endless. One time, we had a hearing to determine if we should have a hearing! Another time, my child's father entered an affidavit because I fed my child ice cream for breakfast! (No one mentioned that the child had a sore throat and this was the only food he could swallow.) Another time, an affidavit was entered because I supposedly fed my child "too many yellow vegetables." From false allegations of abuse to foods, this was a crazy, expensive all-out *war*! Refuse to allow your situation with your child to escalate in this manner. Do it for your child.

My point is that if you do not have your child in your care, it is very important to establish regular contact with your child. This requires much maturity on the part of both parents. It requires you to work together for the best interests of your child. Children have a right to know both mom and dad. (Unless there are specific legal or criminal issues that the child would not be safe.) To deny a child a parent is to deny a child their heritage. It has been my experience that once a parent denies visitation and refuses to follow the court order, they will do it again! Seek mediation if you suspect a problem.

Marry a man with a child from a previous relationship or marriage, and you will:

- Allow for that child's visitation in your home.

- Arrange your schedule around his child's and the mother's schedule.
- Share holidays with his child.
- Learn about the child's grandparents and other extended family.
- Work so he can pay his child support, his child's health insurance, and childcare.
- Be featured in court documents for his child support—i.e. where you work, your job title, salary, assets.

To give you an example, when my former spouse went to court for child support, I was sent papers from Office of Support Enforcement, inquiring if I owned any antiques. They wanted to know my assets—did I own valuable jewelry? Did I have insurance policies? Did my son have a paper route? I used to scoff and remark, "what do they think they are going to do? Make our son with his little paper route, contribute to his dad's ex-partner's child support?" Our son was 4 years old at the time! I used to wonder if my fragile grandmother lived with us, would they figure her Social Security into the equation?

At your partner's child support hearing for his other child, do not waste your time bringing up the fact that you have a child with him. When I tried that, I was told, "you knew those other children were there and you went right ahead and had him!" It was a punitive, very unprofessional remark by a person in authority who should have known better. Apparently, my child did not need to eat, he did not need clothing, nor did he need a roof over his head. The Child Support Officer just demanded to see our joint income tax return and snipped, "we will just take 49% of *this* income to pay for his child support."

After we divorced, I had to fight battles to collect child support for my son, while the State aggressively collected child support for his dad's other children. Here I was working my behind off to support my child while the ex-wife sat on welfare producing babies, with people jumping to help her! Where is the logic? What happened to my marriage? Why was I so full of hostility? I didn't know when I entered into the relationship with this man that it would be like this. People rudely said, "you knew what you got yourself into" or "you made your bed, now you can lie in it." I read a highly recommended book, *Second Wife, Second Best*, and had a clearer picture. No, I did not understand it would be this way. This was supposed to be fun playing "mommy" to his kids. And you think you will have some power? The only people with power here are the court system and the mother of his child.

I know I am talking about issues that are boring. I know that right about now, you are ready to probably doze off! If it is this boring just *reading* the pages, just think how horrible it would be if you had to *LIVE it* every day of your life! Now there's a challenge…!

Chapter 5

There is never a "perfect" time to have a child. If everyone waited until the "perfect" time to have a child, they probably would not have one! Our population would be greatly reduced! Sure, you may not feel ready for this, but few people are when the event happens. Some people may seem more maternal or paternal, more nurturing, or better able to instantly connect with babies, but parenting can even be difficult for them.

A baby is not a "band-aid" for a relationship. It will not "seal" your love, or "trap" a person into marrying you. Giving birth to a guy's child will not make him love you. This baby is not going to grant you instant acceptance into his family. Situations like the 20-minute sex act on the beach and the payment for 18 years are true, but extreme cases.

First, let's talk about your habits. Do you smoke? If you do, envision a cigarette hanging out of your baby's mouth. Imagine the pure, innocent, and sweet smelling baby with black lungs. Every time you smoke around your baby, the baby may as well take a few puffs of your cigarette too. Second-hand smoke is a killer. Your baby is an innocent bystander—helpless to make its own decisions.

The baby depends on you for the very air it breathes. You are going to be a parent so it's time now…it's time to stop that smoking! Let your baby breathe clean air and have healthy lungs. Your baby will love you for it!

Do you consume alcohol? What about other drugs? Habitual drug use can cause many negative outcomes. First, any type of drug can alter your behavior. Do you become violent when you drink? Do you suffer from "road rage"? Have you operated a motor vehicle while drinking? Do you pass out? Do you like to get high with the music blasting? Well, this cannot be tolerated by a baby. Your change in behavior due to drugs can be unpredictable and the volume can injure the baby's hearing. I have heard many teens talk about their boyfriends and how abusive they can be. They have a short fuse, so to speak. The smallest thing or incident sends them into orbit and they blow. If you choose to make a baby with a person with this characteristic, you are bound to have trouble. Why would you think a person who becomes violent or has an anger management problem will make a good parent? Do you think they will suddenly stop being abusive when they have a child?

I recently talked with a mother who was so distraught because the father of her baby would not acknowledge the baby. He had not been to visit in 3 years and the mother was upset. She told me how he is an alcoholic and is "crazy." She said he is unpredictable, manipulative and rude (typical characteristic of drunks). My question to her is why? Why would you want this monster around your child? Even if he does visit, he will probably then want to take the child in the car. Do you want him driving the baby in a car when he is drunk? What if he goes into a "black-out rage?"

This young man can benefit from a visit to a Detox Center, where he can talk with alcoholics who have gone through alcohol withdrawal. They can tell him firsthand about the "DTs" (shakes), hallucinations, and near heart attacks, seizures, etc. associated with your body withdrawing from alcohol. It is an ugly place to be. Withdrawal can take anywhere from 24 hours to days. In short, withdrawal is hell on earth.

Many things go into making a baby. What do you know about the other partner's health history? I know of a nice guy who fathered a child. He met the young lady and it was instant attraction. Lust, desire, passion...it was rampant. They *had* to be together. It was instant sex and immediate parenthood. She told him she loved him. Of course, she told him she was using birth control. She had never met anyone like him. He was the man she had been waiting for her whole life. Being the responsible guy, he made plans to marry her. He eagerly awaited the time he would go to the obstetrician's office to the unborn child's medical appointment. The mother of the child kept stalling, and making excuses for him not to go to her pre-natal appointments. Despite his pleas that this was *his* baby too, she would not allow him to go. She made appointments, and canceled them as quickly. Their conversation became a whirlwind of lies, deceit and juggling obstetrical appointments. In his own secrecy and deceit, he learned the date of an upcoming appointment and went to the office. It was not until the doctor mentioned the risks to the baby coming down the birth canal during an "outbreak," that the father-to-be even had a clue of the real issue. This beautiful, sexy, young lady had "assaulted" this guy in her own way. She knew she had the Herpes—she just neglected to mention it to him. Strapped now with Herpes for life, the guy knows he paid a tremendous price for his passion.

For the rest of his life, he will be cautious of sex partners, monitor his body for "outbreaks," and watch for side effects from his medication. He no longer feels sexy or desirable as he constantly fears he will pass this disease on to a sexual partner. This has affected any future relationships he will have, and he still to this day—5 years later—cannot begin to fathom this. But…she said she loved him. You do not "assault" someone with a disease out of love. She knew exactly what she was doing. He trusted her with his life.

When you make a baby with someone, you rarely think to ask if diabetes runs in their family. How about cancer? Other life-threatening diseases? You should be informed about this so you can give the information to the child as they grow into adulthood. When you bring a human life into the world, you owe it to this child to be informed about his or her health history. Is the child pre-disposed or are there genetic factors to certain diseases or conditions? You need to now learn the child's other parent's family heritage as this information is a vital part of your child's identity.

Life will be different. Your friends will understand that you now don't have much time to spend with them. As a matter of fact, you may find that they are not coming around as much as in the past. They do not enjoy watching you change a diaper, or enjoy looking at you with baby spit on your collar. Babies vomit, pass gas and get colic.

I remember the first time my baby screamed all night several l-o-n-g nights in succession. I had never heard of the term "colic." I learned all about it, as I did "croup" (a viral infection). There were endless nights of "croup," steaming out in the shower, and listening to my baby cry like a seal. Every time your baby becomes ill, you will need to have good medical insurance. They also require "well baby check-ups," with immunizations and physical exams, as scheduled. As a parent, you will become educated about the schedule. You will not have the money to spend like you used to, and the little free time you have, will now be spent sleeping. This goes double if you find yourself being a…(gasp!) SINGLE PARENT!

It is okay to be a single parent! I will not kid you, it is hard work. It is no easy task to be mom and dad. There are single parents that blow it off and say, "it's no big deal," but don't believe it. Accepting the responsibility and doing the work of two parents can be challenging and oh, yet so rewarding! I do not believe that a living situation is necessarily better for a child simply because mom and dad are in the household. There is a popular national radio talk show host who promotes the philosophy that every child deserves a two parent household. I agree with this, however, it is not always feasible. What if one parent in the two parent household is being abused? What if the two parent household is constantly in turmoil? What if the child is growing up amidst constant fighting and screaming? A one-parent household may not be ideal and perfect, but it can be peaceful. A single parent can focus more of their time and attention on a child—thus, not sharing their time nurturing a relationship with a spouse or partner. This same radio talk show host scoffs at daycare and lays a guilt trip on working parents who place their children in daycare. (We single parents have enough guilt, thank you very much.) During one call, when a young mother was talking about placing her child in daycare, the host quipped, "I feel so sorry for that child. Her mother wants to farm her out to an institution!" Do not believe this garbage. Single parents can have enough guilt trips without feeling bad because they have to utilize daycare while working. Children gain social skills interacting with other children. The daycare experience can broaden their creativity, help them to make friends, and be in a structured environment.

One opinionated mother told me her children had never seen the inside of a daycare. She added, "besides, they do not do anything there but tie children to chairs." *What?* So, she collects welfare—years of collecting welfare, as each child is born.

Placing your child in daycare? You then have a responsibility to place your child in a safe environment. You must visit—several times, unannounced. Check the daycare provider's credentials. Call the Daycare Referral Line through your State Department of Social and Health Services—or your State agency, to find out if the daycare has state violations. When was their last inspection? Research this. It is well worth the time and will afford you peace of mind. Your child will be in this environment for many hours a day so remember this when you are inspecting. Is it a cheerful place? Are there safety precautions around stairs, shelves, stove burners, etc.? Watch your child interact with the provider. You will give a better work performance at your place of employment knowing your child is safe.

As a single parent, it is tempting to jump into a relationship with a financially secure person who enters your life. I have seen single women make this mistake. They are so busy grasping onto their "knight in shining armor" who comes along to rescue them, that they rarely see the person's flaws. Oh sure, marrying someone to provide for you and your child may appear to upgrade your lifestyle. I know of many single women who jumped into the first relationship so they could move out of their dingy apartment and move into a nice house. Hooking up with a rich person can afford your child the finest education in a private school. Having a partner to depend on and to pay the bills certainly beats working two and three jobs to support your child! If you are afraid to live on your own and be independent, this seems like the solution, or answer to your prayers! Remember though, this is not about you anymore. It is about your child and would this decision be the best decision for your child?

Be cautious of men who enter your child's life and become an instant buddy. He may seem like a tremendous help, he is always there, and willing to baby-sit, but these can be major tactics that child molesters use to get near their victims. As one child molester explained, "I gain the mother's trust. I seek out a single, struggling mother. Often times she has many children and her hands are full. I offer to lend a helping hand. I do fun things with the children and take them off of her hands. She is grateful and begins to depend on me more and more. I wait for that one opportunity…and I *will* have that opportunity." It is not up to someone else to raise or discipline your child. Just be careful and trust that intuition.

Several years ago, a millionaire entered my life. Oh…the answer to every woman's dream. He was handsome, educated, loved rock music, and he was lots of fun! I met him when I was 18 and we dated. Our paths crossed again 25 years later. We went out to dinner a few times. I noticed he had a few deep rooted prejudices and made rude comments about his beliefs. He was condescending to me and treated me at times like I was an idiot. Once, he got upset with me because he thought I was rude to his dog! This man's priorities in life centered around one person—himself. He boasted about building another home that sat on a hill overlooking the city. He would repeatedly tell me "the city lights are so bright through the skylights at night, that you do not even have to turn on a light to go to the bathroom!" He offered to give me an endless supply of money to furnish his new home. The sky was the limit in being creative, decorating, and spending money. He told me I could have "all of the fun in the world!" Yes, that's my idea of fun—decorating his house. He treated me to the finest of things, and the most expensive restaurants. What was wrong with this picture? Even when I tried to tell friends that I did not care to see him again, they were shocked! One friend remarked, "what can be so wrong? Joy, you have had to work your entire life…your child would have everything…the finest of schools. You would never have to work another day in your life!" I know of several women right now who would have grabbed this man, moved their children into that beautiful home with the skylights, and who would be living a grand lifestyle. Well, here I sit exhausted, in my modest surroundings, with no regret. His money was not the issue. The issue with me was how he would treat my child. From this man, my child would learn prejudice. He would learn terms such as "spic" and the horrible racial, black "n" word.

My son would see a "rich bigot in action" and I would fear he would grow up to exhibit the same warped opinions. I will dwell in my modest home, continue to work until I am exhausted, drive my simple car, and be alone. The millionaire in this scenario is not the man with the house on the hill overlooking the city.

Who is rich? My son and I—for I had my priorities straight and I could see the "danger signs."

I am not going to be with a partner just so my rent can be paid, my child will be fed, or I can live life a little easier. I am not going to marry a man so he can discipline my child because I need a break. I will not allow a partner to beat my child or myself. I will not seek someone out so they can financially support my child. My child does not need a man to "play daddy." He has a biological father. I will not allow my child to see a man in my bed. My child will not see me be fondled, nor will he be introduced to an array of men. I will not immediately introduce my latest date or his children to my son so we can all instantly become "one big happy family." My son will see me in a healthy, progressive relationship that moves through the proper steps. He will learn respect, commitment and love from my examples. In return, he will hopefully one day, in his adult life, have secure, stable relationships as a result.

What will your priorities be in a relationship? What will your actions in a relationship teach your child?

Chapter 6

I do not want to bore you with every detail of a lengthy story about me. Besides, I have already written a book, *The Fourteen Year Hour*, about my horrendous experience. I would, though, like to share kind of a summary of my ordeal.

At age 20 I met a man who was 10 years older than myself. I knew him for 9 months and we married. I was not in love—you know, that giddy feeling we have when we see the guy. If I had to use one word to describe myself during this time, the word would be "immature." I did not fathom the depth of the seriousness of standing before God and taking wedding vows. I thought of how we would live in the beautiful lakefront home with the dock. How we were going to Nevada for our honeymoon. How I would be "taken care of," and would never have to worry about money. Events took a strange twist…

- At age 24, we had a son
- At age 27, we divorced (our son was 3)
- At age 6, my son was paraded into a therapist's office where he said I abused him. The therapist told me to stay away from my son—"children do not lie about

abuse."

- My name was placed on a State Registry as a "substantiated" child abuser, although an investigation was never conducted and no one ever contacted me.
- I was facing a felony and possibly prison.
- I took a polygraph test, which indicated I was innocent.
- My ex-husband took a polygraph and it indicated he had sexual contact with our son.
- At age 28, I entered into another relationship with an alcoholic, which produced one son. I was like many women—I believed the alcoholic would change. I just knew he would keep his promise to go to A.A. I attended Al-Anon meetings. (He did not ever go to Alcoholics Anonymous and still drinks to this day.)
- When this relationship ended, this second man became best friends with my ex-husband.
- The father of my second child now said I abused our son also.
- When my son from the second relationship was 3, I lost custody of him when a "default" was entered in court—my attorney failed to appear in court on my behalf. My son was returned to his father and was later discovered to have sperm in him. If you know your biology, then you know the sperm did not come from *me*.
- This father warned my family and I, "you are never going to see the kid again."

My first son was one day gone at age 6 and I have not seen him since. Today, he is 25.

Raised in an environment of "brain washing," hatred

and violence, this son grew up to be an abuser and drug addict.

My second son was gone at age 3 and returned to me at age 16…a stranger. He is 21 today. He was told throughout his life that I am "evil" and that my family and I would harm him. He survived years of endless, continuous abuse—episodes of which he video and audio recorded. (I have seen and heard the episodes.)

I was court ordered—or forced—to pay money disguised as "child support" to my younger son's father (approximately $17,000.00—$8,000.00 in one lump sum, and paychecks that were garnished over a 5 year period).

It was later admitted that the entire fiasco of my son being supposedly abused by me was made-up. It cost me years of humiliation, I nearly lost my social service career, and I suffered estrangement with both of my children. I survived years of knowing my children were being abused. I felt powerless, and the experience helped to shatter my faith.

I accept responsibility for my mistakes:

- Wrong choices in a partner
- Not taking responsibility for birth control
- Believing I could change an alcoholic
- I did not have college, a stable work history, or life experiences and could not take care of myself
- I believed a man was "going to take care of me"

Why are we a society that condones child abuse? I think

about this often. We pour thousands of dollars into child abuse prevention programs yet we do not take a closer look at the courts. Some family court commissioners are appointed—not elected. They sometimes refuse to consider all of the evidence—in child custody cases—especially evidence of abuse. This, of course, results in not only unfair rulings, but potential harm and risk to your child's safety.

Guardian Ad Litems (volunteers) who are supposed to remain "neutral and in the best interests of the child," sometimes are in reality opinionated and take sides. If you think that since he or she is a drunk, uses drugs, and your friends tell you, "there is no way in this world that drunk would get custody of your child," you better think twice! Drug users and abusers are granted custody of our children every day in the courts! I recently read statistics that indicated *70% of abusers who want custody of their children, are granted custody. They are experts at making their victim—the one they abused, appear crazy and unstable*. There are web sites that address this subject. You should be very concerned about this.

His "partying" may be cool now, but it won't be in a different time. If you have had a child with him, he can be granted "visitation" with the child. He will pick the child up sometimes every other weekend (or as court ordered), and your child can be gone from you for the weekend. Some non-custodial parents also have contact with their children for half of the summer, holidays, etc. Is he still driving drunk? Using cocaine? Blacking out? It didn't bother you much before but it will now. Your baby will be in his care—drunk or not, high or not, and he can do anything he pleases. Does he have a "short fuse"? Hope he doesn't lose his temper with the baby. Hope he is one of the parents who return the child to you at the end of the weekend. Believe me when I tell you some parents literally kidnap their own children! Hope he is not seen as a fit and proper person to have custody!

There could come a time when the courts and the law cannot protect you and your child. You made a baby with him—your baby's father is *one half* of your baby's identity. You don't want him in your life now? Too bad. He has rights! I speak from experience—years of court battles and worrying about my son's safety. The battle, the expense, the stress, the agony…it made me old before my time.

Someone recently wrote me asking for advice. She was upset because her brother was a drunk and violent. She was mad because he has only seen her two children twice, and has never seen his own baby. Why in the world would she want a person so violent around her children and his own? So he can injure the children? Drive them recklessly in the car? Why would you *want* this? Think about it. The children are innocent and they depend on you to protect them. She is upset because her brother does not come around children with his drunken, obnoxious behavior? Oh, her feelings are hurt…

Another person asked my advice in a similar situation. His mother and father had beat him frequently as a child. He went on and on about how his feelings are hurt because his mother and father hate his family. He complained that they have nothing to do with his children. If they beat him frequently as a child, does he want them to beat his children also? Have they changed? Have they both attended anger management? Have they attended therapy to find out why they are so abusive? He is hurt because his parents won't come around his children. Perhaps this is a blessing in disguise.

One woman wanted advice from me because her fiancé hates her children! Your fiancé hates your children and you are going to marry him? I would not even consider marrying someone who hated my children. Is this a set-up for abuse or what? How long do you think it would be before this new husband would be beating her children? Why is she interested in a man who hates her children? This marriage would be for mom…certainly not what is best for her children.

A stepmother pushed her step-daugher. I do not have clear details about why she shoved her, other than her husband—the father of the girl—called the police and had his wife arrested. Dad was so concerned that someone would shove his child. Yet, he did not do a thing when he had known all along that the cousin of the child's mother has been molesting the child. If you can call the police for someone shoving your daughter, why can't you file charges on a pervert who is molesting her?

A friend of mine was married to a man who beat her for years. When I say beat her, I mean he broke her jaws, arms, etc. For fun, he would knock her teeth out, or call her "whore, bitch" and other assorted names. She stayed with him for years, and endured each beating. Her mother told her "he is really not that bad. He just works hard and is tired." Her other girlfriend told her "he really is a good person, underneath it all." Her daughter and son dreaded the beatings. When it was Christmas, or whenever everyone would try to act like a "typical family," the children would hug and kiss dad at mom's command. They were afraid of him, after all, they saw firsthand how violent he could be. They became the "little peacemakers"—they did literally anything they were told to do, to keep peace. Through the years, their parents eventually divorced, and the children went with dad "on visitation." Mom did not tell the courts he was a batterer, so she did not request "supervised visitation." The children went with the monster, as they were instructed to do. They did not stand a chance of escape from this abuser. Mom made sure they were right there…in his home…in his rages and in his violent clutches. She told her children that the batterer loved them. She told the children she loved them. The daughter ran away numerous times and ended up on drugs. The son became suicidal.

I know of several women who have allowed each boyfriend who comes along to beat their children. I know of one woman who had 2 children with behavior problems and her children drove her crazy. So, she married and now *he* is in charge of her children.

One mother of two knew a man for a brief few months, and uprooted her children to be with him. She suddenly removed the children from school and they went off to live in the wilderness. They lived secluded and hidden, with the stranger. No one really knew the man but one onlooker told me that she met him at Christmas. She shook her head and said, "he could not stand being around her sons. They just drove him insane." Choosing to move and uproot your children like this was a decision made more for mom's enjoyment than being the best thing for the children. These children were separated from the only school they had ever known, their friends, their grandparents, and their community. Upon returning to civilization, two years later, Mom abruptly married the man she had broken up with—prior to meeting her "mountain man." She had told me 2 years ago that this man she married had cheated on her and was an alcoholic. He was violent and full of rage. She now lives in her beautiful, magnificent home with the view, which she boasts to everyone. When asked about the boyfriend and the years the family was in seclusion, one son only says, "he was going to build us a house and we learned to shoot guns." No one really knows what happened and it is not discussed.

A woman I used to work with—I will call her Molly—asked me if I would do a "background check" on a man she was involved with. Let's give him a false name too. Let's call him Elmer. She was not just beginning the relationship but was already intimate with him. He had been around her children, slept over at her home and was trying to make himself be a permanent fixture in her home. Why wouldn't he? While she was at work, he was sleeping in, having friends over, and eating her out of house and home! I agreed to do the background investigation. (A dear friend of mine Michael Starosky of "The Detectives" Investigation Agency in Seattle is a Private Investigator who "showed me the ropes" in investigating people.) It only took about a half hour to read the man's convictions. Elmer had been in some trouble, that's for sure. When

Elmer's cousin was accused of raping a woman, Elmer threatened the victim and her children. He discreetly warned her, "if I were you, I would keep an eye on your children. You better watch them when they are going to and from school." Elmer—suave guy that he is—has numerous charges and convictions—mainly in the domestic violence arena. He beat a woman in south Seattle—repeatedly ramming her head into a coffee table. The victim tried to phone 911 but he began beating her again—dragging her into the bedroom. As the telephone receiver fell to the floor, 911 traced the call to the small residence. Elmer has threatened relatives, women he was involved with in relationships and co-workers. As I investigated, I learned there were even more charges against Elmer at another courthouse/justice center. Not needing to read more of the abuse, and immediately determining that Elmer was going to eventually assault this woman and her children, I suggested we leave. On the way home, Molly was quiet except for asking one thing, "can we go see what other court papers there are in Kent?" (a nearby city). Astounded, I looked at her and snapped, "you haven't seen *enough*? What part don't you understand? The guy is an abuser, a batterer and you and your children are at risk. How much more do you need to see before you realize the guy is going to hurt you?" She put her head down and inquried, "don't you think we could go see the other papers too? I can't believe he did all of that. He's just so nice." Of course, Molly had to then mention to Elmer's sister that we were at the courthouse. It was only a few hours before Elmer sat his lady down and "confessed the truth." He admitted to all of the domestic abuse charges, spilled his heart and guts, and added some tears to the performance. You bet he told the truth! He did not have much choice because he suspected his girlfriend knew what he was really like. He emphasized, "I am telling you this because I am so honest and I love you so much. I would never lie to you or hurt you." Do the "con men" come any better? It was on this day that Molly realized what a gentle, caring man she had in her life. She was impressed with his courage and honesty. She kept saying, "He didn't have to tell me all of that but he did…it took alot of courage and I have to respect him for that." I shrieked, "He told you all of it because he knows *you know*. He would never have told you if he were not forced into it!" Molly and Elmer have been together for 2 years now.

Will the sons of these dysfunctional relationships grow up to batter? Will the daughters grow up to choose partners who beat them? After all…they learned it from the parent! Do they know any other kind of life? Will the cycle of abuse continue? What do you think?

A single, teenage parent recently confided to me, "I sometimes want to hit my child out of anger and impatience." She said, "I feel sometimes like I am going crazy. He will not stop whining. He cries all night. I just feel like sometimes I am losing control." Children need to be taught, have things explained and be corrected several times before they develop a certain pattern of behavior. A forceful slap or violent shaking that is later rationalized as "discipline" (when the parent calms down), can slip into a habit of abuse.

These are excellent examples of how we acquaint our children with abuse and/or abusers, and how we fail to keep them away from abusers. The children grow up to abuse and "parent" the way they were parented. Think about your choices. Put your child's best interests first.

Never, *ever* shake a child. Do not ever let anyone shake your child. To do so can result in Shaken Baby Syndrome. This is a serious acquired, traumatic brain injury caused when a frustrated adult shakes a child. The child is usually less than 1 year of age, and the adult shakes them to make them stop crying. Although this frequently occurs in children less than 1, there have been documented cases of Shaken Baby Syndrome in children as old as 5 years of age. Typically, the child is held by the arms or trunk and shaken in a back and forth or "whiplash" motion with repeated force. When a child is shaken, delicate veins between the brain and skull are ruptured and begin to bleed. As blood pools between the skull and dura (tough, fibrous membrane that lies next to the brain), subdural hematomas are formed. These produce pressure that along with the natural swelling (edema) of the bruised brain causes damage to brain cells. Once brain cells are damaged, they are never regenerated or replaced. In addition, the swelling and pressure causes the brain to push and squeeze down on the brain stem which controls vital functions such as breathing and heart beat. If the swelling and pressure are not controlled, vital functions will stop and the child will die.

Symptoms of SBS (Shaken Baby Syndrome) include very mild forms of irritability, poor feeding, vomiting, and lethargy. Serious symptoms include breathing difficulty, seizures, coma and death. Children with any of these symptoms should receive immediate medical attention.

SBS is diagnosed through x-rays of the head using a CT (computerized tomography) Scan, an MRI (Magnetic Resonance Imaging), and an eye exam. X-rays are often done on the rest of the child's body to determine if there are any past or present bone fractures.

Courses of treatment consist of medications to reduce swelling, and surgical methods to relieve the pressure caused by subdural hematomas. Vital functions such as breathing are usually taken over by a respirator. Studies suggest 15-30% of the children die. Remaining survivors often suffer varying degrees of cerebral palsy, paralysis, seizures (epilepsy), blindness, deafness, and learning or behavior problems.

Shaking a child…it is not something we think much about. It can be deadly. Whether you are baby-sitting or caring for your own child, *never shake a child.* Do not "rough house" with your child. To be real safe, do not bounce a child on your knee or toss them in the air. If your partner has difficulty controlling anger, he or she will not make a good baby-sitter. This is common sense stuff!

Parenting is an incredible responsibility. We must do everything in our power to keep our children safe.

Chapter 7

In the greater Seattle area, we are fortunate to have an agency such as DAWN—Domestic Abuse Women's Network. DAWN is a non-profit organization in South King County. They strive to help people create healthy, peaceful lives no matter what their circumstances. With a 24 hour crisis line, emergency shelter, client advocacy, women's groups, legal advocacy, children's programs, teen advocacy, and community education and outreach, DAWN provides confidential services. There are no fees. You can call, visit, or pick up one of their brochures (usually available at the public library). Most cities have an agency similar to DAWN. Check your local yellow pages and see if they have some services that are right for you.

If you are presently in a relationship, what is happening? Is this a fulfilling, healthy relationship? Do you feel there is something "just not right"? If you feel there is something wrong...there probably is. It is the same philosophy for alcoholics—if you feel you have a drinking problem...you probably do!

In your quiet time, answer these relationship questions: Is your partner attempting to control and manipulate you? Are there emotional putdowns? Physical assaults? Sexual pressures? These are some of the tactics that are used to gain control. To gain control of you. Violence is not macho. The relationship seems better today…it was worse yesterday. Tomorrow it could be either. It is like a constant roller coaster ride. Do you feel…

- confused about your relationship,
- like you are going crazy
- that you are "walking on eggshells"
- that it is difficult for you to spend time with family or friends
- that you cannot do anything right
- that your partner decides when and where you have sex
- that you are in a relationship with two completely different people
- that you need to justify everything you do?

Does your partner…

- call you names or put you down?
- change the rules on you?
- want to know what you're doing and who you're with all of the time?
- act extremely jealous?
- find excuses to keep you from getting enough sleep?
- push, shove or grab you?
- keep you from leaving when you want to leave?
- force you to do things sexually you don't feel comfortable doing?
- promise to change (get counseling, go to A.A., etc.)

There are subtle tones of abuse everywhere we turn. It appears people are attempting to incorporate it into romance and childrearing. Imagine for a moment how confusing and frightening an environment with the above mentioned tactics, feelings. etc. would be for a child. Our children watch us and they learn from us. We are the example.

The other day, I turned the TV on to a popular daytime soap opera. The woman was sitting on the bed, draped in a sheet. The man was bragging about how their sex was so incredible the night before. She swept her hair out of her eyes, appearing nervous and upset. She hung her head and quietly said, "At first it was a little weird." The camera focused on the bruise on her arm. She added, "Things got a little out of hand last night." Her partner's response? He grinned and reminded her, "*That* is because you drive me wild. I just could not hardly control myself you are so irresistible." A few scenes later, the woman appeared dressed and ready to leave his apartment. He was strutting about the room, offering her donuts and being "affectionate." At first she refused his affection, but he began to slowly stroke her hair with the brush. He caressed her hair, with his gentle, massaging fingers. His hands delicately rubbed her neck. She began to feel a bit turned on…and then made a horrifying statement. She apologized, "You know, I did kind of overreact, I am sorry." They began to kiss, to fondle and yearned for each other. There she stood, displaying the bruise he inflicted upon her…all in the name of "passion and ecstasy." This is absurd and it is an outrage. Those same fingers connected to those same hands are the weapons that assaulted her body. There is absolutely nothing romantic about this.

It is not a compliment that a man gets so carried away with his orgasm or pleasure that he bruises you. There are obvious violent tendencies within him. He is not loving, he is dangerous.

People rarely fall in love with their rapist. Another daytime TV program features a long-term relationship. The couple met when he originally raped her. They are a popular item on daytime soaps. People love them! Do long term viewers remember how they met? Can't they still hear her screams when he raped her? Why do we glamorize or make something romantic out of his violence?

In the above scenario—or in any heated, escalating situation, a woman has the right to say *no*. It does not matter if both partners are naked, within an inch of each other, throbbing, and ready to have intercourse. It is important to assess the situation, and listen to your "gut" feeling. That "gut" feeling or intuition will *never* let you down. It is okay to say no. You should not require permission.

Hopefully, the woman in the first scenario will not return for more abuse. When she left the apartment, though, things were pretty sensual. She will be back…be back for more of his "uncontrollable passion." She should have had him arrested and thrown in jail!

You may wonder how you would defend yourself. This reminds me of an uncomfortable situation a young lady found herself in one evening. Simply put, she changed her mind. They had spent quite some time turning each other on with foreplay, and she suddenly decided she did not want to do this. He was becoming quite ro aggressive. She did the first thing that popped mind! She fell to the floor and pretended to have some sort of "seizure" or "attack." She moaned, groaned, made strange looking faces, and you know what? It worked! It certainly broke the mood, and he opened the door. He was genuinely afraid of her and what could happen next. The combination of an adrenalin rush and intuition can save your life!

There was another situation in which a man broke into a woman's home. His apparent motive was sex. She heard the noise outside the window, froze and called 9-1-1. The glass shattered and to her horror, the man came through. He immediately began removing his belt, he commented that he was "horny," and it was obvious that she was going to be raped. He did not seem the least bit interested in her possessions, valuables, etc. So…she handed him the telephone and ran. The voice on the end of the telephone was sexy, inviting, and ready to give phone sex. He did not know who was on the other end of the telephone and he did not care. He had phone sex with her…she tantalized him with the most provocative words. His intended victim—the occupant of the home—was hiding. The police soon arrived to arrest him. He had just had phone sex with the 9-1-1 operator! What a smart, quick-thinking 9-1-1 operator! She saved a woman from being raped!

Chapter 8

WHO ARE YOU? You are so much more than a name, a grade point average, someone's daughter or son, or someone's girlfriend or boyfriend. People have spent enormous amounts of money in therapy, trying to discover exactly *what* makes them tick! Yes, people 40, 50 and above wonder not only who they are, but what in the world they are doing here!

Have you ever thought about what makes you happy? Where are you going in life? What do you plan to accomplish and how do you plan to get there? Are you just drifting through life aimlessly, or do you have a purpose? Are you invincible—hey, nothing can harm *you*! Are you invested in your community and family? Is home a place where you connect with family, or do you just use home as a place to eat and sleep? What makes a happy home? What do you do that brings happiness to your home environment and others? What kind of parent do you plan to be? What are your principles? Would you give up your life for your beliefs? Where will you be in 5 years? 10 years? Do you pray? Do you read the Bible? Do you attend church regularly, or do you attend church only during holidays?

Life is hurried. It seems like there is always temptation to take the convenient or "quick" way out of a situation. This can be deadly. Allow me to give you an example. In a time of choice and "it's *my* body" attitude, we can justify doing away with a pregnancy pretty easy. Often times, the woman is more concerned with having the money for the abortion, instead of the life long effects. Sometimes the father of the baby will readily come up with the money. Sure he will…it relieves him of any responsibility. Just pop a pill and have a spontaneous abortion. Just schedule an afternoon appointment at the clinic and you can "put all of this behind you." Any partner who pressures or attempts to persuade a woman to terminate a pregnancy against her wishes, cannot care much. It is shocking that too many women are coerced into doing this, without full understanding of the consequences and long term effects. This is hardly an informed decision. Do not—I repeat, do *not* make your choices based purely on emotion or fear. Do not allow anyone to persuade you to do *anything* that is against your values.

A few years ago, I knew someone who had an abortion. Despite my pleas to not do it, she decided to have this done. Additionally, I was put in the awkward position of giving her a ride to the abortion clinic. At first, I told her to get her own ride—I believe my comment was "get your own ride to go kill your baby," or something similar. I was rude and so cruel. She quipped, "I am going to get there whether you take me or not!" I saw her tears and tried as best I could to be supportive. When she called the abortion clinic to tell them I would be bringing her, the receptionist was cheerful. The physician's office has never been near this cheerful when I went in with a cold! We were warned to not bring any children to the abortion clinic. I should have asked the receptionist why. Are they afraid a mother might change her mind? The woman repeated, "No children in the clinic, period." They were so afraid...so intimidated by the presence of a child. Why, it might save a life! Wouldn't that be dreadful?

Of course I am being sarcastic! Or am I? You know, though, children are everywhere. Even after she had the abortion, she still had to adjust to seeing children. Abortion, I say, is like the popular saying regarding suicide, "a permanent solution to a temporary problem." What happens when your personal situation improves? When you are married? More financially and emotionally secure? When one day you join the church and your religious beliefs strengthen? As one teenager sobbed over the telephone after her abortion, "*What* have I done?" This is irreversible.

I still shudder at the woman who was so starved for attention that she made an appointment to have an abortion one afternoon. She wanted him to notice, to come charging after her, to "rescue" her. She was positive that this would jolt him into caring. This baby's life hung by a thread...she repeatedly glanced at the door. He did not come on that afternoon. Feeling betrayed, hurt and resentful, she terminated her pregnancy. At 16 years of age, people tried to console her by telling her she would have other children. She did—6 others, but none of them replaced the one—that first baby. She had many children—oh how she tried to move on. She took drugs to numb the pain. She chose abusers, and she hated herself. Her relationships with her children are strained and stressful. Even in a house of children, she feels alone. She is not though.

We have a forgiving God. We are not perfect, we are sinners. We all make mistakes—some of these are huge. God forgives, but can you forgive yourself?

Long after that abortion, that guy you thought loved you just may be gone. Will he care if you have post-abortion complications? Will he care if every year for the rest of your life you think of that baby at its birthday time, on Mother's Day and at Christmas? Don't think your mother and father won't think of this. After all, that baby girl or boy was their grandchild. We are talking family here. Boyfriends come and go. If a guy wants you to undergo this procedure to keep him, let him go. Eventually you probably will say good-bye anyway. The person you must live with and see in the mirror will always be *you*!

As a woman who miscarried twins, I will tell you that I will always remember. The exact dates and my dreams for my babies will always dwell within me. The blood kept coming for a week. The flow grew increasingly heavier. With my daily physician visit and blood draw, I searched the doctor's face for a ray of hope. Who were they? They were frail. They were partially formed. They fought hard, and they clung to me. They just could not survive. There is a corner of my heart reserved for my tiny daughter and son. Through the years, I imagine how old they would be, what they would look like, and what kind of relationship we would have. On occasion—on the anniversary of my miscarriage—I have had vivid dreams of my daughter. Abortion proponents will tell you they were "fetuses" and not human. My personal feeling is that I did not bond with anything *but* my children. They had no sex organs, but they were my daughter and son. How did I know I had a girl and boy? A mother knows. This is not the "mother-fetus" bond…it is the "mother-child" bond. These were the children that the Lord gave to me. I may have carried them for a brief time, but they have impacted my life for eternity. They were God's creation—perfect gifts. They were a part of me in 1986 and they are a part of me today and tomorrow. Many people believe the death of a child is life's greatest pain and tragedy. Just believe this.

When my son entered the 7th grade, I was informed at the school assembly that my son could go into the local teen health clinic and receive a variety of services. These services—including birth control, can be given without my permission. I do not even have to be informed. When I was 14, I was a giddy, immature, weird, total brat. The thought of having the responsibility to terminate a pregnancy, obtain birth control that has many side effects, etc. is at least absurd. Talk to mom and dad! Talk to an older sister, an aunt, a favorite teacher, a pastor or a school counselor. Talk to God. If you do not know Him, get to know Him. You do not have to make such huge decisions on your own. I assure you, your family members are not being nosy, or trying to bother you. We parents call it love. Communication truly is the "anti-drug" as the advertising says, and you must talk with them too. It works both ways you know!

Where does God fit into all of this? I hope in the center of your world! As a child, one of the very first of the Ten Commandments I learned was "Thou Shalt Not Kill." What about this could we possibly not understand? Where is God? You tell me! If you are lying with your feet in cold, silver stirrups, ready to have a suction device inserted into your vagina, it is not too late! Ask God for guidance. Pray. You would not be the first woman to leave an abortion clinic with her baby growing in her womb! When you eventually hold your baby in your arms for the first time, you will have no doubt you did the right thing. This moment will be as close to "heaven on earth" as it gets.

There is not a man on this earth whom I would choose over my own child. If he walks because you cannot abort the being inside you, consider yourself lucky. The mere *suggestion* that you have an abortion says a lot about *him*. Can you love someone who does not value human life? Be honest. Caring about a person for their money and security they provide, the sex you have together, and the status of being "his" does not count! Can you love this person, inside and out…the person who wanted you to have an abortion? Can the same hands that offered you money to go the abortion clinic caress you and make you feel good? I doubt it. When your baby is learning to walk, starting kindergarten, and riding a bike for the first time, you may see your baby's father's face. With contempt. But you will see it.

We simply cannot just make situations, things—and above all, people—just disappear. Creative advertising makes abortion seem affordable and convenient. There is so much propaganda out there, it is difficult to know what to believe. One side says it is a fetus—it is not a baby until so far along in the pregnancy. The other side says it is human being from the moment of conception. I don't know about you but I call a heartbeat, and a kicking, breathing being with a blood stream a baby. There may be thumb-sucking happening in your uterus, or kicks. You feel it. With this being comes past generations of heredity and genes. What is *not* human about this?

Fortunately, we live in a society today of increased open adoptions and special arrangements. Today, mothers can literally choose the adoptive parents for their baby. They can receive baby pictures, attend birthday parties, and have ongoing contact with the adoptive parents. Doesn't this seem like a much more healthy attitude for everyone concerned? I commend mothers who give their children to adoptive couples for the child's best interests. This has to be the most unselfish act in the world. I wish we could have a special "Mother's Day" just for these mothers. They certainly deserve it.

If you believe you could benefit from attending church, speaking with a pastor, or by obtaining counseling, do so. The strongest people I know are not afraid to get down on their knees and pray, read the Bible and recognize that they need professional help. Problems do not simply fade into the night. They fester, as a small flickering flame.

The bottom line is that you must make the choice that is right for you. Our choices usually affect others. Somewhere, this "fetus" as proponents of abortion refer to, has a grandmother, grandfather, aunt, uncle and cousins.

Value family. If you pose nude for *Playboy* or strip in Las Vegas, your child will live with your choices too. Consider family when making your decisions, but still do the right thing for you. It is difficult. You know, though, regardless of your past choices, Christians know we receive grace and forgiveness.

Chapter 9

Regrets. Do I have regrets. Yesterday, I was 16, strolling the halls of high school, shopping at the mall and anticipating my life. I awakened one day and I was in my 40s. I do not want to see you one day turn 40 and wish…wish you would not have squandered your life away…wish you would have done things different…wish you had made healthy choices. Time is precious and it can seem fleeting.

I spent exhausting years trying to make dysfunctional relationships work.

So much time has passed amidst my heartache. As you get older, you will reach a point where you evaluate your life—where you have been and where you are going. We make a mistake and we want to put it behind us and move on. We seek closure. We want it to be over, tightly bundled, and tucked away. Sometimes, though, we have unanswered questions, and we yearn for logic in our life experiences. There are just those experiences in which we cannot explain, or make sense. Sometimes, it just is not there. We cannot always tie up those loose ends with curly, colorful ribbons and be done with it. Sometimes we just have to gracefully accept what has happened and attempt to move past it.

I look at people who bring children into this world, and who do not have any idea of the responsibility, and the consequences. Although none of us have a crystal ball to see into the future, the most loving couples can break up. I promise you that having his baby is not going to make him love or stay with you. Don't ever put this tremendous burden on a precious child. The most caring, kind people can end up in a child custody battle. Very unfair, ugly things can happen to good people. I still cannot believe:

- That there are divorced mothers who would make their children sleep in the car to prove their father has bankrupted them.
- That a divorced parent will drive their automobile into the ex-partner's living room.
- That a divorced parent will burn down the ex-partner's house.
- That a divorced parent will recruit others to participate in a "campaign" against the other parent. (Never, ever do this by joining such a group.)
- That there are partners whom, after the delivery of the baby, want sex. *Now*…even though the doctor has told the woman she needs 6 weeks to heal from the stitches. There are partners who will make your life miserable if you do not have sex…it does not matter that your body may not heal and you could be open for infection. If you are with a person who pressures you for sex—regardless of the fact you need to give your body time to heal after childbirth…more important, if you "give

in" and use sex to shut the person up and get them off your back, you do not need to spend another day with this person. This is not a healthy relationship. It is solely based on his needs. It is destroying your self-esteem, provided you have an ounce of it left!

- That there are parents out there who promise to take their child to a football game and do not show up.
- That there are parents so drug dependent, they will steal the child's daycare money out of the jar on the kitchen counter, to purchase drugs.
- That I was ignorant enough to believe just because a father does not take care of his other children, means he will want to take care of our child.
- That I believed an alcoholic's meaningless promises that he would change—despite the "black-out rages," irrational/unpredictable behavior, and the fact the alcoholic had no desire to change or seek professional help. I actually believed an alcoholic could just suddenly quit drinking! I did not understand about the uncontrollable shaking, possible convulsions, seizures, hallucinations, and the process of alcohol/drug withdrawal. It is ugly.
- That mothers honestly believe when they lie down and make a baby during a "one night stand" that he will want to commit to the next *18 years* of supporting that child. He only wanted *a few minutes* with you to have sex. He wanted to have a good time and your body afforded him that. Why does it surprise these mothers that he now runs?
- That my son was severely harmed physically,

emotionally and I suspect sexually, by a parent to whom the courts awarded custody. I am not blameless. No one forced me to have sex with him—this was my choice in a partner. He may have hid his abusive tendencies to me in the beginning, but I still had a choice.

- That I spent so many thousands of dollars on attorney's fees fighting battles for my children, that I could have purchased a house (or at least placed a hefty down payment!)
- That my cute, sporty car was repossessed because I could not make the payments. I had to give all of my money to my attorney to keep fighting for me so I could defend myself against bizarre false allegations.
- That my father told me in 1985 that he never wanted to hear from me again until I let a drunk (my son's father) see my child on an unsupervised basis. My father meant it. I have missed him terribly during the past 17 years.
- That a child I gave birth/life to could be manipulated at age 6 to say I abused him in a one-hour therapy session. It would take years to fight, years to prove my innocence, and a lifetime before it was revealed that the entire fiasco was "made up."
- That I did not use my time and energy that I wasted on these men, to make myself a better person—i.e. pursuing an education, gaining a stable work history, developing job skills, etc.
- That because of my poor choices, I have put my children, my family and myself through a living hell.
- That I had to explain my wrong choice in a partner when I was 20, and the consequences of this, to a man when

I was 42. I will never as long as I live forget his stunned, shocked and puzzled expression. The man I fell truly in love with for the first time in my life, one day disappeared after our slow, progressive 2 ½ year relationship. This is what it feels like to have your heart crushed into a million pieces. My choices—and more importantly, outcomes and end results could have just been too much for him to fathom.

- That parents choose to not see their children. Children have a right to know their heritage and identity. Children need and deserve to know both parents.
- That parents cannot be adult enough to put their emotions, differences and hostility aside for the sake of their child.
- That I was forced to pay a grand total of approximately $17,000.00 ($8,000 00 in cash and garnishments over a 5 year period) to a child abuser.
- That an abuser has the nerve to promise, "it will never happen again," and that the victim truly believes it!
- That a man will quickly re-marry, have a new pregnant wife, and attempt to gain custody of a child based on the fact "we are now a family unit. My new wife will stay home with the child" (while the custodial mother has to work). The custodial mother will be accused of choosing her work over her child and neglecting her child. (If she sat on welfare not working, they would condemn her for this too. She can't win.) A biological mother does not nurture and carry a baby in her womb for 9 months so the new wife can "play mommy" and enjoy the child!

Accept people. Really accept them the way they are. If they tell you they are not going to be religious, they do not want a relationship, or they are never going to marry you, listen to them. As soon as you become determined that you are going to change them, or you are not going to listen to what they are really saying, you have set yourself up for a lot of hurt. It is commendable to believe people can change (and many do), but they are not going to do an overall change in their appearance, personality, morals, value system, and character just because of you. You should not have to change for him either. If it does not feel right…it probably is not right! Love does not hurt. There is not a man or woman alive who is worth stripping you of your self-respect, self-esteem and dignity. You are much too good for this!

When you are loved, your partner will not need to change you, worry about your dress size, tell you what you need and don't need, boss you, or pressure you to have sex. He will be too busy (and *very* happy!) accepting you for the wonderful person you are! Your opinions and ideas will matter, and he will respect you as a person.

If we never made mistakes, life would be pretty boring. If we made no mistakes, we would never learn, never grow or ever be challenged. Mistakes have a purpose in our lives. Decisions come in all sizes—i.e., what will you have for dinner today? Make a bad choice and you may end up with indigestion. Should you go to school today or should you skip school to stay home and sleep? Make a wrong decision and you may go to the principal's office or be found "truant."

Should you have sex with her tonight? Be honest with yourself! Do you have a wedding ring on your finger from the lifetime commitment you have made before God? Are you prepared to pay at least 18 years of child support? Are you capable of putting your child's needs before your own? Do you want to see the child's mother and her family for years to come?

Chapter 10

There *are* healthy and realistic things you can do for yourself.

Get involved. Join your youth group or church! Go on a missionary trip to Mexico or another country and meet new people! I know a man who went to Mexico and assisted in building houses for homeless people in poor villages. Another man visited a poor village there and handed a child a candy cane. The child did not know what to do with the candy cane. Both men say their experience changed their lives forever.

Bond with your community! Attend City Council meetings. Attend any community events—whether it is a summer festival, a street fair, or a public meeting for a released sex offender who is about to be your neighbor. Become familiar with all of your community resources. Read your local newspaper so you know what is going on in your community. Offer to write an occasional guest column in the paper—giving a younger view of an issue. Are there homeless people in your community? The kindest gesture—from buying a person a cup of coffee to a smile—can go a long way. Learn about issues that affect people your age, in the community, look at yourself and ask…what can I do to help and get involved?

Vote. Know the issues, and take a stand.

Be an organ donor.

Volunteer. Opportunities to volunteer are endless. Volunteer at City Hall, the hospital, the homeless shelter, the battered women's shelter, organize a food drive, tutor a child, become a mentor, visit your local animal shelter, get involved with a local crisis line and hear some real life problems. Give a single parent in your neighborhood a much-needed break by offering to watch their child for a while. Play "Santa" for a needy family or "adopt" a child at Christmas and shower the child with gifts!

Visit and learn. Pay a visit or volunteer at a medical clinic where infants are going through drug withdrawal. If you know someone going through residential drug treatment, visit him or her. You will meet people who have gone through drug withdrawal. You will gain increased knowledge and awareness of what drugs *really* do to our bodies. Anyone who has truly kicked a drug habit—whether it be alcoholism, cocaine or heroin, are to be commended for they have been to hell and back. Visit your local library. Read. Visit a therapist or counselor if you feel this would benefit you.

Learn from our wonderful senior citizens. If you want to take a journey into history, visit a senior! Whether you go to the senior center, to a nursing home, or visit in their home, they love to share incredible stories of yesteryear. When I was the Director of Social Service at a long-term care facility, I used to have the sweetest patient. She was incontinent, forgetful with dementia, could not tell me what she had for breakfast this morning, or even her name. She would tell me in detail about the births of each of her 11 children! (And we think we have it rough when we give birth! Listen to *these* stories of childbirth!) When I worked at my local senior center, I had a blast! Talk about wild fun and parties! They taught me the classic tunes and the great bands from yesteryear. I even got out on the dance floor and learned those magnificent dance steps! The seniors would fly on a plane called "Jackpot" to Nevada where they would spend hours gambling! That airplane—with its colorful, crazed design, looked well…a bit scary to me, as it sat alone at Boeing Field. When I told one lady that I would be afraid to get on it, she giggled and said, "Honey, when you are as old as I am, nothing scares you!"

Senior citizens today are a young, vital group—especially to our community. Their contributions to our community are generous. I promise you that you will learn a lot from them.

Learn how to save a life. Register for CPR/First Aid classes through your local fire station or hospital. Learn infant and child CPR. Keep all certifications current. Learn about toxins, houseplants, etc. that are poisonous and post the Poison Control Center telephone number on your refrigerator.

Keep yourself healthy. Exercise, practice healthy nutrition, watch those cholesterol levels, take vitamins—if warranted, learn stress management, do not pollute your body with drugs and nicotine. Have regular check-ups and physicals and see the dentist as recommended. Know your body and be aware of possible signs/symptoms that do not "feel right" and could be indicators of an oncoming illness. If you need help with any kind of problem—whether it is substance, an issue that requires counseling, medical problem, etc. confidential help is a telephone call away. There is no shame or embarrassment in seeking help…it is a shame to not do this. Build on your strengths—not your weaknesses.

Education. Keep your mind sharp, nurture it, and challenge it! Get that education, take those classes you always wanted to take, and offer to share with others what you have learned. Take parenting classes, learn to correctly budget your checkbook, put even a few dollars aside each month in a saving plan—if at all possible (or another time when it is possible). Get in touch with your "learning style." There is no one right way to learn. Each of us has our own way of learning. For example, when I wanted to learn the computer, I took a class. When a friend wanted to learn the computer, he read a book. When another friend wanted to learn the computer, she taught herself. I learned that I couldn't learn computer by lecture, or in a classroom environment. I cannot read a book, go over to the computer, and start applying what I learned (like my friend did). I learn visually and by "hands on"—I have to explore. I learned real quick where to go and not to go in my computer journey. Through making mistakes and repetition, I pretty much taught myself, the way my other friend did. She is now an office manager of a large firm and has never had a computer class in her life! How do you learn best? Learn self-defense techniques. Learn the definition of an "enabler." Do not be one. Do not enable another person to drink or use other drugs by excusing their disrespectful or abusive behavior toward you. Do not call in sick for them, and do not tolerate their rude behavior. Read parenting books and take parenting classes. Be strong enough to ask for community resources or any kind of help when you need it. For some people, it takes alot of courage to ask for help.

Make a vow to yourself. Decide to really listen to people. Especially listen to people whose opinions differ from yours. Through your kind words and actions, you will show others consideration and respect. Vow that you will trust your intuition. If *any* situation, for whatever reason, does not feel right…it probably is not right. Our intuition—that "gut feeling" in our stomach, those subtle vibes or voices we feel or hear…*will not let us down*! Go with the intuition! Arm yourself with this intuition, knowledge and faith. Vow to care less about what others think of you and care more about how you feel about yourself. Be the first to say "I am sorry" and mean it. Stop and really think about your decisions and consequences of that decision starting today. Vow to be the best you can be.

Refuse. Refuse to drive a car or be a passenger with anyone who is under the influence. Refuse to pollute your body by doing drugs, smoking, or engaging in risky behavior. When you drink or take drugs of any kind, it lowers your inhibitions, which can lead to even death. Refuse to take risks with your health and your life. Refuse to allow another human being to hit or assault you in any way—whether it is physically, sexually or emotionally.

Refuse to do this to another person. Refuse to go along with the crowd or be talked into *anything* that makes you uncomfortable. Refuse to compromise your morals, values and beliefs for *anyone*.

Accept that there is no such thing as a perfect parent. One day if you become a parent, you will understand this. You will not be perfect, no matter how hard you try. However, if you look back on your parenting skills—and your life in general, ask yourself one question. *Did I do the very best I could do at the time?* If you answer yes, kudos to you! As you accept that parents are not perfect, look at your own parents because you just may see them in a different light. Embrace your parents, kiss them, give them the biggest "bear hug" in the world, listen, give your time and energy, and most important…not only tell them you love them, but *show* them. *Do it now.* You may not have another opportunity. Life is so precious and it can end in a split second. Love is ageless and priceless.

Respect and obey the law.

Thank God. Be humble, smell a rose, and become enthralled in the twinkling stars. Be thankful that you have eyesight and cannot only see the world's beauty, but be surrounded in it. If you have a home, heat, food, clothing, and you are not sleeping in the cold, dark street tonight, you are blessed. Be thankful for your negative experiences as well as your positive ones. Pray. Pray. Pray.

Understand the correlation between your choices, consequences and responsibility. You will ultimately be responsible for yourself.

Do not make abuse acceptable. Abuse is not sexy, cute,

or usually a one-time, isolated incident. Don't blame his or her abuse on a tough day at work, stress, or accept personal responsibility for abusive actions. They are adults and it is about time they start acting like it. They do not have the right to assault or abuse others. Oh…and once again, this is *not* love.

Do not base your relationship with your partner on the premise that your partner will change. If you are smart, you will accept the person for who they are. You can wait forever for someone to change…and what a waste of your time! *Someone once said, "Choose your life mate carefully because from this one decision can come 90% of your happiness or sadness."* Sure, no one but *you* is responsible for your happiness or sadness. However, if your partner kidnaps your child, abuses or kills your child, beats you, or makes your lives a living hell, this could certainly attribute to at least 90% of your happiness or sadness. There are women who have endured 5 emergency room visits, 4 broken arms and jaws, and they have attempted to flee their abuser. The abuser finds the victim—hunts the victim like an animal. The anger of this perpetrator knows no boundary—even toward an innocent child. The victim obtains a "restraining order" from the court, which may offer a sense of protection or safety. In reality, the restraining order is a piece of paper.

Do not be in a relationship because you need your bills paid, or a sitter for your child. *If you suspect* your partner is an alcoholic or other drug addict, an abuser, or pedophile (child molester) your partner *probably is*!

Set life goals…where do you want to be 1 year from

now, 3 years from now, 5 years from now? You can get there! Keep your faith, learn to forgive others, and hold your head high…no matter what mistakes you have made in your life. There is only one "you" and you have a lot to offer this world!

Ask…if you need help!

Only do things that make you feel good about yourself!

Choose your friends wisely. They say you are judged "by the company you keep." I don't know about that but I do know of innocent people who were falsely accused of crime—they associated with the wrong people. Since their friends did it…people assumed *they* did it. It is called "guilt by association."

Sex can be expensive, and you could pay with your life, or that of your child's. The basic cost to raise a child to the age of 18 is an astronomical $180,000.00! When you check your wallet for the condoms, you had better check your funds! Now *that's* a lot of money!

There is not a lot of purpose in dwelling in the past or looking back, unless it is to focus on your growth. We cannot change yesterday. We can apologize until we are blue in the face, but it will not undo our past choices. When you are contemplating *anything*, stop a moment and ask yourself…*what **positive** can come of this?* You know, I used to begin telling some of the shocking events of my life by explaining, "I really am a good person." This is pathetic. I should not have to say this. I know I am a good person, and I know the truth. I no longer work hard to "convince" people I am a "good person." If I have to try so hard to impress someone, or persuade them to care about me, perhaps I do not need them in my life. The people I have loved who walked out of my life forever, because of my poor choices years ago, are the ones who lost. Perhaps they did not deserve *me*!

Life's experiences are often our best teachers. I am honored that you would take time out of your busy schedule to read about these unforgettable life experiences. A gigantic, intriguing world is awaiting you and there is absolutely no limit to what you can accomplish! My wish for you is that you are close to God, you are healthy, you always strive to do the best you can at the time, you are strong and above all, happy.

You have a life to live to the fullest, so reach for those stars! Be proud of the person you are and go do something spectacular!

Now This is Hot!
And Then He Kissed Me

After such a serious book, I would like to share something whimsical, light, and well…cute! Do you remember your first love? You know, that freckle-faced person who just sent your heart a-fluttering? Well…when you saw *her*, you became all red-faced and began to stutter. When she saw *you*, she ran to climb the nearest tree! You became even more infatuated! She was a challenge! It could have been 3rd grade, or it could have been 6th. Anyway, you knew this was it! True love. I hope you have a "first love" in your heart and that you hold onto the memory. It will only grow stronger.

I remember my first love…and what a love. I yearned for him, scribbled his name in my notebook, and twirled my blonde hair. 6th grade. Ecstasy.

First love. 1965. Enticing, exhilarating, fresh and wild! Is there anything like it? Feelings surge to a place they have never gone, hearts open and flutter, and the spirit comes alive. It is our first introduction to those zany, powerful hormones! He was handsome, that guy of mine! He walked with an air of confidence only a 6th grader could muster. His neat, short hair was always precise, as was that adorable smile he often tried to hide. While the other people at recess played "four square" and tetherball, I often daydreamed. My mind would race to him, my eyes dart to his, and I was oblivious to my classmates jumping rope. I would twirl my flaxen blonde hair, stroke and play with my silken mane. Our eyes would meet for a split second, as the humid heat beat the pavement, but I would quickly look elsewhere! Daydreams rushed in…he was gallant, he was magnificent. One day I just knew he would grow up to win a Nobel Prize! There was nothing this man of the world could not accomplish.

The best was yet to come for there was a surprise about to come my way!

I may have been "boy crazy" but this was one guy who was about to stand out from all of the others. He would definitely move up a few "notches" on my scribbled "boy list." He often rode his bicycle to the nearby shopping plaza, but one of these trips had a specific purpose. He carefully selected the merchandise, after gazing through the assortment. Oh, I had been there, eyeing the jewelry. My girlfriend and I were regular visitors to Woolworth's, trying on "pre-engagement" rings. He probably coyly looked about to make sure his friends did not see him. Wouldn't that be the most embarrassing thing in the world? If his friends saw him, he would just die! He carefully considered his money situation—it wasn't like he had a job that paid a regular salary! He did need to spend his allowance the following week on a new tire for his bike. He frantically again counted his change for the third time. He was about to make the purchase of a lifetime.

He spontaneously, gently placed the ring on my bony finger. Then he kissed me. This was true love because I was heading into orbit! I hoped I was not coming down with something because I sure felt warm all of a sudden. Did I have a fever? I had felt okay until now…dizzy, elated, and flushed, I suddenly had a case of the "giggles." I ran to the nearest tree after he rode off on his bicycle and climbed…high…wrapping my skinny legs around every winding branch. Ouch! My toe got stuck in that one tight squeeze. I held on with one hand, then no hands! I was in love! The 10-carat diamond made me a new woman. My girlfriends were jealous with envy and the boys at recess just looked at my new treasure and laughed hysterically.

It did not take much to impress me.

A swing set with a slide, an inviting swimming pool on a hot, humid Indiana day, or a gigantic pitcher of that green Kool Aid would do just fine. Boys? Oh they had a special place in my life…right up there with my *Meet The Beatles* album, Fudgesicles, going to Pizza King and "Big Boy" and Shelly Fabares.

My young man and I "double-dated" with another couple one evening. They were older than us and they repeatedly watched us as we sat in the back seat. As he drove, the man watched through the rear view mirror and his lovely lady kept turning back, "Aren't you going to tell her how beautiful she looks this evening?" My date carefully repeated the words—"You look beautiful this evening." I saw brilliant fireworks and the twinkling stars I wished upon that night, seemed unusually bright. I knew he spoke straight from his heart. I affectionately batted my "baby blues" at him. I mean I was pretty mature—I was allowed to wear hose on special occasions! I held my head high as we headed down Madison Street. I pretended I was in a chariot. I glanced at my date. Oh, I felt so grown-up and elegant—I was Cinderella alright! This was even better than going to the fair! There was not a double-ferris wheel or roller coaster that could top this feeling! I was dressed in the nicest attire—my mother had helped me with my hair. I marveled at myself in the bedroom mirror for quite some time. I posed, I added a hair bow, I removed the hair bow, and I imagined myself with a grand, sparkled tiara on my head. I was the princess and he was my prince charming! Okay, so my date was not old enough to have a driver's license and the other couple was his mother and father!

At age 12, I had not mastered the art of masking my feelings or playing hard to get.

Just call me a "heartbreaker" or a "diva"! We were, of course, too young to comprehend the true meaning of commitment and promise, so our union was based more on imagination. I imagined being beautiful. I watched every Miss America pageant with wonder, because I believed one day that would be me wearing the crown and jewels! I practiced the walk. I imagined my coiffure, my high heels and my bouquet when my name was announced! Imagine being able to be an adult and being able to do what I wanted to do, with no rules! As "If I Fell" played, I rocked back and forth to the Beatles. I listened to the Beatles, and the Dave Clark Five wondering what it would be like to meet them. What would life be like one day with a husband and children? I just wanted to grow up!

The relationship did not last for the eternity I envisioned. Our "going steady" arrangement met it's challenge—the teen years. Oh, I saw him occasionally, passing in the halls at school, but well…I had moved on! I mean, my friends and I were looking for a more sophisticated guy who was maybe even a few years older! We studied the artistry of make-up, paying much attention to our blue eye shadow and fine eyeliner. We huddled in a small bedroom, as we perfected the latest dance steps. We were future stars of the "lip syncing" crowd—belting out tunes by the Supremes, Petula Clark, and Lesley Gore. We stepped out to every dance and made our grand entrance to every ball game—loudly cheering! Bicycles and tree climbing were no longer the "in" things to do.

New friends and dating became the core of my life. My former elementary school boyfriend and I remained friendly—as people often do after a big "break-up." I soon moved on to the man of my dreams…and the next…and the next. Eventually, in 1970, I moved away from the Midwest to Seattle, where I would begin my junior year of high school. It just did not seem important to look back.

Looking back on first love. 2002. Through the years, I sometimes thought of that elementary school youngster and how he and I must share an identical yearning to return to that time of innocence. We would meet again. One day. I believed he must have the same fantasies as I. Where is he? What does she do for a living? Does he remember the evening of our first (and only!) date? With each passing year, I thought of him. With each milestone, he wondered about me.

Who could forget the mementos—the awkward kiss, the act of "going steady," the department store ring that was worth its weight in "pixy stix" and Tootsie Rolls, and the laughter? These tokens are priceless—these memories that creep into my quiet, private thoughts.

In 1965 life was supposed to be carefree and fun. It was. In 2002 life is supposed to be more serious. It is. When I used to wave to the small planes passing overhead above my Muncie backyard, I never thought of bio-terrorist attacks or threatening crop duster planes. When my young man tenderly planted that kiss on my lips years ago, our world felt secure. We had not known destruction so I could not fathom twin towers collapsing. Horror, insanity and violence were strangers to me, as they should be. The only mask I ever considered owning was a Halloween mask—certainly not a gas mask. I never gave thought to bombings while doing cartwheels across the lawn. My friends and I slept outdoors in a tent all night and we did not know families who had security alarms. The world was a nice, safe place and I could not envision it being any other way.

My teenage son believes I grew up in "the old days." He sometimes asks, "What did you do back then?" He asked the other day, "Did you have TV?" He repeatedly asks, "You really did not know who was calling before you picked up the phone?" No, and as I repeatedly tell him, we did not "click a mouse" to visit our friends…we actually saw them face-to-face. Besides, if someone dared to mention a rodent or "mouse" I would have shrieked! When we said we were going to "check the mail" we literally trekked to the mailbox! We had to hold a newspaper and/or book in our hands to read it, and we had to physically visit a library to research a book or topic. No doubt I would have believed "surfing the net" had something to do with a surfboard and water!

What do you say to someone after 35 years? He instantly referred to me as a "goof." Yes, that was he! Didn't he call me that in the 6th grade? My son asked, "What's a goof? Something weird, no doubt." I smiled. "No, honey, something affectionate." My former heartthrob apologized when the moment finally came, to rid himself of a guilt and burden he had been saddled with through the years. Although he claims he "ignored" me when we were high school sophomores I do not recall this.

Although life is now dominated with the hustle and bustle of raising children, working and paying bills, we still laugh with a pinch of that too familiar childish silliness. We suddenly have perfect, crystal clear recollection of those special years. Regardless of the past years, or the others who came and went in our lives, our bond is permanent. He will always play a part in my life, whether it is for his boyish charm, or his nervous kisses.

No matter where our paths have led or where we have been, there is a certain sprinkling of magic in the world reserved for just the two of us. I will never giggle quite like that little girl again. I will never display such impish behavior as climbing those sprawling trees. I will never feel so unencumbered and so free to be me. Me. Career woman and social worker, blonde-haired flirt with pigtails. Community volunteer, hip, single mom to my teen, published author, who used to wear white "go go" boots! A woman of professionalism, who once upon a time would just "die" if she did not have a blue "madras" shoulder bag. Yes, I did don the striped red/blue/green mini-dress and pink hot pants, much to the delight of every hormone raging teenage boy! That was me, appearing "ghostly" under that white lip polish and if I were to wear that "Slicker" lip tint with my business suit today, people would think I am anemic! If you could muddle through the three layers of eye make-up, you would eventually find those buried blue eyes. Although I still have the blonde hair, I no longer wear it in a "flip" or "pageboy." It has been years since I attempted to iron my hair, "tease" it, tape my bangs or sleep in black brittle hair rollers. If I slept on those rollers now, I would have a migraine for two days!

We were always in a hurry to grow up. We tried to look older, act older, and lived for the day we would turn 18! Graduation came and went. Now, can we rewind back to the time when romance began with "Once upon a time…" and ended with "And they lived happily ever after"? Where there is no responsibility, no debt, and no pain from valuable life experiences. For a day…for a moment? Our various schools do not exist as they once did, but we can still clearly envision them. If we could only be that little girl and boy, laughing, kissing, and being our genuine selves. In my heart of hearts, I know it could never be like the first time and that is what makes it so precious. We had our time and what a time it was…

We are all capable of giving and receiving love at any stage of our lives. Most of us have a "Kenny" or a "Joy" in our lives. Who is to say we were not in love? Do we have to be a certain age to be in love? When love is tender and inexperienced, is it any less love? Where is that person? How is that person? Most important of all, is that person healthy and happy? It is a universal curiosity. You may meet again one day, via telephone, through letter, at a class reunion, or over the computer. I still remember my *Weekly Reader* in the mid 1960s and its prediction of future high technology. By 1970, we would be able to see each other when we talked over the telephone. People oohed and awed…this was predicted to be the sensational height of technology in the future! We never dreamed of a Microsoft Corporation or the concept of instant messaging. It would have been difficult to conceive that one day we would just "click" and begin to converse over a computer screen. If you are blessed enough to be in one another's lives, years later, however this may occur, your curiosity can finally be put to rest.

Once upon a time there was a girl and boy who fell in love…. Adolescence? A crush perhaps?

Something happened in that magical era for here we are many years later, often discussing our families and jobs.

I did not make Miss America, nor did he win the Nobel Prize. He has not purchased a ring from a five and dime Woolworth's store for any other person but me. I have not "gone steady" with anyone but him. Some things are meant to only happen once in a lifetime.

Only one thing, though—I sure wish those white "go go" boots would come back in style! I could wear those just one more time…now those were groovy!